BOOK ANALYSIS

By Jim Hilton

Brighton Rock

BY GRAHAM GREENE

BrightSummaries.com

GRAHAM GREENE

ENGLISH WRITER

- **Born in Berkhamsted, Hertfordshire (United Kingdom) in 1904.**
- **Died in Vevey (Switzerland) in 1991.**
- **Notable works:**
  - *The Power and the Glory* (1940)
  - *The End of the Affair* (1951)
  - *Our Man in Havana* (1958)

Graham Greene was one of the most revered English novelists of the 20th century. He was known for his expert blending of plot and weighty ideas, writing novels that were both exciting to read and thoroughly literary. Fascinated by political intrigue and the international order, Greene travelled widely, and set his novels all over the world, from Mexico and Cuba, to South Vietnam and Sierra Leone. Greene was a convert to Catholicism, and this religious sensibility infuses many of his texts, particularly *The Power and the Glory* and *Brighton Rock*. Greene was also a lifelong devotee of the movies, and spent years writing film reviews for *The Spectator*. He also wrote film treatments and screenplays, including one for Carol Reed's acclaimed film, *The Third Man* (1949) featuring Orson Welles (American actor and director, 1915-1985).

BRIGHTON ROCK

A TRUE MASTERPIECE OF PSYCHOLOGICAL SUSPENSE

- **Genre:** thriller
- **Reference edition:** Greene, G. (2004) *Brighton Rock*. London: Vintage.
- **1st edition:** 1938
- **Themes:** violence, love, Catholicism, social class, sex

Brighton Rock was Graham Greene's eighth novel, and it remains one of his most famous. First published in 1938, there have since been two film adaptations made, along with multiple adaptations for stage and radio.

Unlike Greene's later more globe-trotting yarns, *Brighton Rock* is set almost exclusively in the Brighton of the 1930s. Beneath the fairground atmosphere of Brighton's pier and promenade, and the happy swell of day-trippers down from London, Greene's story focuses on the undesirable, criminal element at work in the town. Our anti-hero is the 17-year-old Pinkie Brown, or as Greene often refers to him, the Boy. In the wake of his mentor Kite's murder, Pinkie is busy settling scores and consolidating the now leaderless mob under his own control. But as the murders begin to pile up, Pinkie finds himself drawn into an intensifying spiral of violence that demands more and more victims. Determined to stop him is the unlikely figure of Ida Arnold, a sentimental and unstoppable woman with a strong sense of Right and Wrong.

SUMMARY

PART ONE

The scene is Brighton, and it is the Whitsun bank holiday. Charles Hale, or Fred, as he is also known, works for the *Daily Messenger*. He's the 'Kolly Kibber', paid by the newspaper to tour a specified town and deposit his calling cards. If a member of the public recognizes him and speaks the right words – "You are Mr Kolly Kibber. I claim the *Daily Messenger* prize" – they win ten pounds, or if they find one of his cards they win ten shillings (p. 4). However, Hale has a history of involvement with the Brighton mob, and now he is convinced that his old colleagues mean to murder him. One of these is a 17-year-old boy, Pinkie Brown. Hale becomes more and more paranoid: he is too afraid to go to the police and too afraid to try the train station. He bumps into a woman called Ida Arnold and sticks by her desperately, hoping that the company of a witness will keep him safe. Ida insists on leaving him alone for a moment while she uses the lavatories. Hale urges her to be as quick as possible, and promises to be waiting by the turnstile when she comes out. When she does come out, he has vanished.

The Boy, Pinkie Brown, meets with his mob associates in a café on the pier to check that Hale's murder went according to plan. One of his men, Spicer, has continued to deposit the Kolly Kibber cards around town, so that Hale's time of death will be placed later. In the manner of Kolly Kibber, Spicer has also placed one card in a random restaurant café, underneath a tablecloth in Snow's. This angers Pinkie, who realises that if a member of staff finds it, they might realise that it wasn't the real Kolly Kibber who came in. Pinkie goes to Snow's himself to retrieve the card, but when he arrives, he finds it gone. A young waitress, Rose, confirms Pinkie's fears, telling him how she found it, and that it was strange that she didn't recognise the Kolly Kibber when he came in. "I've got a memory for faces", she says (p. 7).

Back in London, Ida Arnold hears news of Hale's death, which has been ruled a heart attack. Thinking back to the day she met him, she remembers how afraid he was, and starts to suspect that the newspaper has not got the whole story. She begins to investigate, attending Hale's meagre funeral. She also consults her Ouija Board, which finally convinces her to return to Brighton and solve the mystery of Hale's death.

PART TWO

Pinkie has realised that he must keep a close eye on Rose, the waitress, whose keenly observant nature could expose them all. He meets up with her after work, and subtly warns her about the dangers of loose talk, showing her a bottle of vitriol. The pair then go for a drink at Sherry's and discover that they are both Roman Catholics. Later in the evening, Pinkie and his crony Dallow travel out to a bookmakers' and violently collect their protection money from him. They learn that a rival mobster, Mr Colleoni, is muscling in on their territory.

The next day Pinkie is called in to see Mr Colleoni at the Cosmopolitan Hotel, where Colleoni – rich, sophisticated and European – makes it clear that he is now in complete control of Brighton's syndicate. A policeman apprehends Pinkie on his way out and warns the Boy against initiating a gang-war.

PART THREE

Ida Arnold has arrived in Brighton, and places a bet on a horse, Black Boy, following a tip she received from Hale the day he died. She then goes to Snow's, and begins interrogating Rose about the Kolly Kibber card. Remembering Pinkie's warning, Rose becomes nervous and evasive, which only confirms to Ida that something is afoot. She goes to the police station to air her suspicions, but the inspector remains sceptical of any foul play.

Meanwhile, Pinkie's accomplice Spicer is becoming edgy and afraid that the truth about Hale is going to come out. He is drawn back to the scene of the crime, and the seafront photographer takes a picture of him unawares, looking sullen and mysterious. Rose calls up on the telephone to tell Pinkie about Ida's questioning, but Spicer answers. In his mind, the authorities seem to be closing in, and he dreams of moving to Nottingham and buying a share in his friend's pub. Pinkie meets with Rose again and learns of Ida's investigating. The pair take a bus up to the countryside, and although Pinkie is repulsed by

Rose, he also feels a certain kinship between the two of them, and while there they share a kiss.

Returning home, Pinkie finds Spicer drunk and passed out on his bed. He wakes Spicer and suggests that he needs a holiday. Pinkie then calls up Mr Colleoni, and arranges for Colleoni's men to murder Spicer at the races.

PART FOUR

It is the first day of the races, and Pinkie and Spicer have driven up together. Spicer is in a good mood, oblivious to the plan that Pinkie has set in motion. Pinkie spots Colleoni's men and pats Spicer on the back as the signal. But instead of just attacking Spicer, Colleoni's mob go for both of them, and Pinkie comes to the bitter realisation that he has been double-crossed. He is slashed in the face and the knuckles and flees the racecourse, bloodied and weeping. After hiding out in an old garage, he makes it down to Snow's, where Rose dresses his wounds.

The Boy returns to his digs where he informs the others of Spicer's death, and calls for the lawyer, Mr Prewitt. He has decided that he must marry Rose, as a wife cannot testify against her husband. Prewitt arrives and informs Pinkie that although the pair are underage, a legal ceremony would be possible. Dallow shows up and Pinkie is horrified to learn that Spicer is in fact still alive, and survived the attack. Pinkie wastes no time in finishing Spicer off himself, and soon Spicer lies dead at the bottom of the stairs. Appalled, Mr Prewitt asks how it happened, and answering him, Pinkie breaks some old broken bannisters and throws them down on the body. "These stairs have needed mending a long while," he says (p. 132).

Ida questions Rose further about Hale and Pinkie, but Rose is fiercely loyal and finds Ida's concern repugnant. As Pinkie interrupts them, forcing Ida to leave, Pinkie asks Rose if she would like to marry him, and she says yes.

PART FIVE

Pinkie, Cubbitt and Dallow take a drive up to the Queen of Hearts to toast Spicer, and there they meet Spicer's lover, Sylvie. She and Pinkie dance together, and eventually they go outside in search of a parked car. Pinkie finds Sylvie's liberated and experienced sexuality enrapturing, and yet when the moment comes he cannot bring himself to go through with the tryst. The idea of marriage to Rose now disgusts Pinkie more than ever, but it is the only way of covering up Hale's murder.

The next day Pinkie goes to meet with Rose's parents to obtain their permission for the marriage, and they begrudgingly agree in exchange for fifteen guineas. On arriving home, Pinkie is greeted by the mob throwing a betrothal party for him. He soon takes offence at the jokes being made at his and Rose's expense, and quarrels with Cubbitt - almost telling him the real manner of Spicer's death.

PART SIX

Cubbitt, depressed and drunk, goes to the Cosmopolitan and tries, unsuccessfully, to get a job with Colleoni. While there, Cubbitt meets Ida in the hotel lounge, and Ida finds out from him that Hale was indeed murdered by Pinkie's mob.

Pinkie and Rose get married in the registry office. The ceremony is perfunctory and deeply jars with their sense of Catholic ritual. After a drink, they wander the pier and Rose convinces Pinkie to record a voice message for her on vinyl. Unbeknownst to her, the message Pinkie records is bitter and cruel. They eat some Brighton rock, and finally go back to Pinkie's place, which the mob have all vacated for the night to give them some privacy. After they make love, Pinkie feels rejuvenated and almost ecstatic, but this feeling soon fades. Waking in the night, he feels suffocated and entrapped by Rose's presence in his room and in his life, and he goes for a night-time walk.

PART SEVEN

Rose wakes up alone in the morning, and curiously considers her new life as a married person. Ida comes to her again and once more attempts to convince Rose of the danger she is in and to leave Pinkie. Meanwhile, Pinkie, still fearing exposure from Ida's investigations, goes to see Mr Prewitt. Finding the lawyer blind drunk, Pinkie realises even he cannot be relied upon, and he strongly urges Prewitt to take a holiday in France for a while, and to leave on the earliest boat the next day.

Pinkie also has a plan to be rid of Rose altogether. He means to contract her into a double suicide, although of course he has no intention of taking his own life. After laying the seeds of this idea in Rose's mind, he drives the two of them up to Peacehaven, where he means to carry out his plan.

Pinkie's crony Dallow has until this time remained entirely loyal to him. However, when Dallow hears about the suicide plan, he begins to view Pinkie's behaviour as reckless. Ida manages to convince Dallow that Prewitt has been arrested and that the whole jig is up, and so Rose at least ought to be saved. The two of them, along with a policeman, drive up to Peacehaven and intercept the young couple, just as Rose is pointing the pistol to her head. Pinkie attempts to attack the party, but spills his bottle of vitriol over himself. Fleeing over a field, Pinkie finally disappears over the side of a cliff and is killed.

Ida Arnold returns to London, vindicated in her judicial crusade, having exposed Hale's murder and saved Rose from the Boy. Rose however remains devoted to the memory of Pinkie, and hopes that she carries his child.

CHARACTER STUDY

PINKIE

Pinkie, or the Boy, is Greene's central character in *Brighton Rock* and the novel's antagonist. While we feel for the deeply painful nature of his existence, and the very limited chances offered him in life, it is impossible to condone his actions, which consistently harm and manipulate the people around him. He is ambitious, driven, and resourceful, but he is also insecure, neurotic and impossibly bitter. Almost each and every contact with the world seems to sting him in some way, and enter his unconscious log-book of grievances against humanity. He is a Roman Catholic, but Christ and the potential existence of a Heaven never seem to enter his mind: all he has ever known, and can ever know is Hell. Hell makes sense to him. Punishment, aggression and harsh words come naturally to him, flowing from a childhood which Greene leaves murkily obscured – although we know that Pinkie's parents are dead.

The one childhood memory that regularly comes into Pinkie's mind is his first awful recognition of sex, as he remembers sharing a bedroom with his parents, and seeing the shape and hearing the sounds of their intimacy on Saturday nights. This recollection never fails to breed repulsion in him. He sees sexuality as bestial, and this reaction only further fuels his own bitter self-awareness of his virginity. The Boy, in a mob of older and more experienced men, views sex as just another adult game that the world would rather keep him out of. His indulgent violence, breaching the unspoken code of conduct between mobsters, becomes a form of over-compensation – a way to prove his manhood.

Pinkie's relationship with Rose seems, at times, to give the reader hope for his redemption. There are moments when it seems like Rose's uncritical devotion to him might really melt the icy chill in his soul. Yet the more attached to him she becomes, the more he begins to hate her. She represents the same inexperience and the same working class degradation that he is trying, through his bloody labours, to escape from. While their similarities bond them together in the face of others, Pinkie's ultimate disgust towards himself causes him to also hate Rose, who is like his mirror image. His final gambit and attempt to kill her actually result in his own death.

ROSE

Rose is a waitress at Snow's café, above which she shares a room with two other girls. Like Pinkie, she comes from a poor background, but as a woman, her social fate relies unduly on her romantic decisions. She pours all her attention and purpose into her burgeoning relationship with Pinkie, and counters his callousness, disinterest and disgust with a fierce loyalty towards him. In her increasingly religious mindset, she sees the two of them as damned together. The sacrifices one makes for love turn, for her, into a more profound and significant sacrifice of one's soul for another's.

Rose's class and religious sensibility cause her to clash fundamentally with Ida Arnold. While Ida insists that she is looking out for Rose, and has her best interests at heart, Rose hates the older woman with a passion. Ida's moralising, interloping, do-gooding patronisation infuriates her; it seems to merely chirrup and declare the carefree, struggle-free nature of Ida's more mobile, middle-class life, in which she can hop between towns, and take each day as it comes.

While Rose is certainly a victim of Pinkie's sociopathy, she is far from a weak character. Alongside her seemingly desperate devotion to Pinkie, she retains a striking personal integrity throughout the novel. Her rescue by Ida and the policeman at the end might well have saved her life. Yet we might also read that final intervention as an unwelcome interruption: a denial of Rose's agency, coming as it does just at the very moment when she herself is about to decide what to do.

IDA

Ida is a caring and sentimental soul, and a great believer in life. She likes singing old ballads; she likes drinking Guinness and stout, among other things; she likes a bet every now and then, and every now and then she likes a man. She believes in free and easy living, but that is not to say that she does not have a moral code. She believes in fair play, and she believes in Right and Wrong.

Her moral compass operates on a completely different scale to Pinkie and Rose's, who view the world through a far more ambiguous and inscrutable conception of Good and Evil. Ida's sense of the Right thing to do demands action, and this gives her fuel to power forward in her campaign against Pinkie, while those around her shrug discouragingly. While her conception of life adheres to no strictly religious system, she believes in a kind of afterlife, in which the dead can contact the living, and it is on the strength of a message from her Ouija Board that she decides to return to Brighton.

In contrast to the pained inexperience of the young couple, in which every romantic encounter is rendered by Greene like a kind of awkward skirmish, Ida's attitude to sexuality is open and compassionate. She has a husband – Tom – though the two of them called it quits some time ago. Now she is amenable to companionship where she finds it, and as she says, it's all natural – there's nothing wrong with it. Although she has no children, Greene repeatedly emphasises the feminine curvature of her body and its promise of maternal compassion towards the men she meets.

While everything in Ida's free and easy bearing revolts Rose, Ida – like both the young pair – has an obsessive streak, and it is this which unites all three in the dynamic of the narrative. Ida is not just a woolly do-gooder, but a force of nature. In her own charming way, she is hell-bent on uncovering Hale's murder and on saving Rose, even though she has only a tenuous relation to any of them. She could at any moment pack up and head home to London – and yet she perseveres. Ida undoubtedly emerges as the hero of Greene's novel, and a wonderful foil to his two main protagonists.

ANALYSIS

1930S THRILLERS

While *Brighton Rock* is undeniably a novel with great psychological depth, first and foremost, it is a thriller. From the 1920s onwards, and partly through the influence of the film industry, the culture-consuming public became increasingly interested in dramas focused on the exploits of gangsters. Gangster thrillers would often feature:

- The appearance, or at least the suggestion of, visceral violence;
- Dangerous or exciting sexuality;
- A sense of gritty and specifically urban underworld existence.

In *Brighton Rock*, Graham Greene employs all of these elements, while simultaneously playing with and subverting them:

- Greene's narrative in *Brighton Rock* is saturated with violence, and yet the actual details of that violence are usually left to the reader's imagination. For example, when Spicer is murdered by Pinkie, we don't actually witness the deed itself. Like Mr Prewitt, we simply discover "the body, spread-eagled like Prometheus, at the bottom of Frank's stairs" (p. 132), and infer what must have happened. This is also the case for Hale's murder, in which we can only guess through repeated but elusive hints that Hale was somehow murdered with a stick of Brighton rock. Greene wants to wield the narrative weight of violence, and build a realistic gangster story in which people really get hurt and face real danger, but without openly indulging in the gratuitous enjoyment of violence for its own sake. In the 1930s, American gangster movies had become increasingly violent, while the hard-boiled novels of Dashiell Hammett (American author, 1894-1961) were, by the end, often littered with bodies. In Greene's treatment of violence, we can see him drawing away from this context, and not wanting his novel to be viewed as pure, vulgar entertainment.

- Sex and sexuality do feature prominently in *Brighton Rock*, but again not in a straightforward way. Greene does not paint a glamorous portrait of fast-living and passionate encounters in Brighton's criminal circuit, but instead opts to make his central character a bitter and highly repressed virgin, who loathes the very idea of sex. Around him, the liaison between Dallow and Frank's wife Judy is hardly the stuff of Hollywood gloss either. Even Ida, in her wholesome and healthy attitude towards sex, renders it thoroughly unspectacular, and hardly the stuff of sensationalism. In *Brighton Rock*, Greene is not at all interested in presenting a sexualised aesthetic of the kind that we might expect to find in a paperback thriller. Rather, he is interested in exploring the individual and differing relations of his characters towards sexuality.

- The prime location for a typical story set in the British criminal underworld would surely be London. And yet Greene chose Brighton – the weekend resort for Londoners, and hardly an urban sprawl. But the power of Greene's portrait of Brighton lies in this interface between the cheerfulness, the tourism and seaside, and the bloody struggle for survival underneath. While Mr Colleoni knows only the finest suite in the Cosmopolitan, and Ida only knows the waterfront and the Sherry, and the cosy pubs of Brighton, Pinkie and Rose know the area beyond, behind the picture-postcard festivity and shallow entertainment. As Pinkie walks up the hill to meet Rose's parents, towards his old neighbourhood, "Every step was a retreat" (p. 153). The poverty, which lurks behind every town's smooth façade of gentility, threatens to pull Pinkie back like a chasm, more fearful than the mouth of hell itself. This progress from out of the slums gives urgency and meaning to Pinkie's criminal mission. On no account will he end up back *there*. Far from glamorising the earthy environs of crime, Greene presents characters willing, by any means, to escape from brutal poverty. The real underworld, Greene suggests, is not something romantic or rugged, and not something that we – the readers – want to know about.

RELIGION IN *BRIGHTON ROCK*

Graham Greene converted to Roman Catholicism in 1926, and his religion deeply infuses his two central characters in *Brighton Rock*. Pinkie and

Rose are both Roman Catholics, and this is one of the first facts which they bond over together. For centuries following the Reformation in Britain, Catholic populations faced repression and attendant social hardship. For Pinkie and Rose, their religious and class backgrounds intersect exactly. The intensely personal recognition of pain and suffering which they both share is grounded in their Catholic sensibilities, but also in their mutually difficult upbringings, and the lack of social opportunity and mobility offered to them. Ida's class identity (although she is not wealthy she is certainly mobile) might be read in conjunction with her thoroughly un-Catholic worldview, and her implicitly Anglican or non-religious background.

In Catholic doctrine, the mercy of God is inscrutable and essentially unknowable. Pinkie holds the obscure hope that if the time came, at the very last instant of his life, he might impossibly discover the ability for repentance in himself and be saved – "between the stirrup and the ground" (p. 115). Rose embroils herself more and more with Pinkie, even though she knows he has done bad things, and even goes along with his plan of a suicide pact, hoping that at the very, very last moment she will discover the strength to save herself from him. As J. M. Coetzee (South African author, born in 1940) writes in his introduction to the book, "to postpone repentance until the moment between the stirrup and the ground [...] is a deep sin, a sin of pride and presumption" (p. ix).

Their shared sense of sin locks both characters into a fixed downward spiral. Once Pinkie has got away with one murder, the next leads on quite naturally – and besides, if he is already damned, what does it matter? For Rose, committing sins for Pinkie's sake brings her closer to him, and becomes a strange act of love. Suspecting the kind of evil things he has done, she wishes to be like him – to be experienced. Transgression becomes a key constituent of experience for her, and when Ida suggests that she is an inexperienced child, this only pushes Rose to transgress more.

We need not read *Brighton Rock* as a critique of the Catholic worldview. Ultimately, Pinkie and Rose are immature, frightened and brutalised teenagers without decent role-models, or meaningful opportunities in life. Their Catholicism offers them a way to order and understand the world, but it cannot be expected to save them from it. We get the sense that Pinkie has not been a practising believer since his early childhood, and that were he now to try, he wouldn't know where to start.

FURTHER REFLECTION

SOME QUESTIONS TO THINK ABOUT...

- Can *Brighton Rock* be read as a coming of age novel?
- Pinkie seems to have a different relation to violence than other characters. What does Cubbitt mean when he drunkenly repeats to Ida that "Carving's different"? (p. 177).
- After Pinkie's close shave at the races, Rose cleans and dresses his wounds. What significance might this moment have in a Catholic context?
- What significance does this description of Mr Colleoni have for the wider action and world of the novel?

> "Suddenly sitting there in the rich Victorian room, with the gold lighter in his pocket and the cigar-case on his lap, he looked as a man might look who owned the whole world, the whole visible world that is, the cash registers and policemen and prostitutes, Parliament and the

> laws which say 'this is Right and this is Wrong.'" (pp. 67-68)

- In your opinion, is *Brighton Rock* a literary novel or a thriller? Or if both, how might it deconstruct the binary between the two?
- List some of the literary references Greene uses.
- Do you find the narrator's focus on numerous different characters convincing?
- In your opinion, was Pinkie truly evil, or was he a victim of society?
- What do you think Rose would have chosen to do at the end of the novel, if she hadn't been rescued by Ida? Would she have killed herself?
- In your opinion, if Rose were to listen to Pinkie's recorded voice message after the novel's end, would it change her mind about him?

We want to hear from you!
Leave a comment on your online library
and share your favourite books on social media!

FURTHER READING

REFERENCE EDITION

- Greene, G. (2004) *Brighton Rock*. London: Vintage.

ADAPTATIONS

- *Brighton Rock*. (1948) [Film]. John and Roy Boulting. Dir. United Kingdom: Charter Film Productions, Associated British Picture Corporation, Pathé Pictures.
- *Brighton Rock*. (2010) [Film]. Rowan Joffé. Dir. United Kingdom: StudioCanal, BBC Films, Kudos Film and Television, Optimum Releasing.

www.brightsummaries.com

Ebook EAN: 9782808014601

Paperback EAN: 9782808014618

Legal Deposit: D/2018/12603/490

Cover: © Primento

Digital conception by Primento, the digital partner of publishers.

Printed in Great
Britain
by Amazon

31304825R00031